HAVING
MANIC
DEPRESSION

HAVING
MANIC
DEPRESSION

Hannah N. Walsh

authorHOUSE®

AuthorHouse™
1663 Liberty Drive
Bloomington, IN 47403
www.authorhouse.com
Phone: 1 (800) 839-8640

Published by AuthorHouse 04/23/2015

ISBN: 978-1-4969-5111-3 (sc)
ISBN: 978-1-4969-5113-7 (e)

Library of Congress Control Number: 2015906580

Print information available on the last page.

This book is printed on acid-free paper.

Preface

On November 11, 2011, I put myself into a drug treatment center. I had been on two very bad drugs, although I loved them both: amphetamines and Klonopin. I loved the amphetamines for the surge of energy they gave me, and I loved the Klonopin for the sedation it caused. After using these drugs, it was as if I was ripped from my own biological highs to lows; I could only experience the highs when I was in a manic state and the lows came after the manic state. I have manic depression, and at the age of fifty-four, I had a very long and frightening manic episode. Paradoxically, getting off the drugs caused the very bad manic episode. I had spent three weeks in treatment. The first three days were spent in detox. To help me with withdrawal from the Klonopin and amphetemines, the treatment center put me on liquid Phenobarbital. On my second night I curled up in a ball on the floor of my room, rocking. I had already taken my purse apart inch by inch just in case the treatment center staff had overlooked even *one* Klonopin. They hadn't, and I can only describe what I went through on the floor as another trip through the birth canal. It hurt, and this time I remembered the pain. I was moved to the residential unit on day 4; a staff member escorted me and my black Hefty bag full of my possessions to "the other side."

The treatment center must have been designed by an architect skilled at planning labyrinths. The staff member and I walked for what seemed like forever just to get to the "other side." I sat in front of the nurse's station for about two hours. I watched all the other addicts move around the long corridors and through nameless doors. After two hours, I was taken to my room by a sixteen-year-old girl who was coming off of heroin and Ecstasy. She would show me the ropes. She was very sweet and helpful. She was staying next door, so it worked for the first five days. On one of those days a staff member caught on that she was my "den mother." A middle-aged woman having a teenage den mother was against the center's rules, but we at least managed to break this rule for several days. I didn't like my adult "den mother" much very much and could better identify with the sixteen-year-old, having spent the last seven years of my twenty-two-year career teaching high school English.

At the treatment center, you spend much of your time in 12-step meetings, and the 12-step meetings at this center were phenomenal compared to the more staid meetings on the "outside." Every speaker meeting was held in the big cafeteria at seven o'clock in the evening. The addicts who spoke at these meetings delivered their messages in what can only be described as the most exciting way possible; my mind was just snapping every night after these meetings, which caused me insomnia. My insomnia was so bad that I didn't sleep for nineteen days. The night spent in detox on the floor was a sleepless night, for the most part. The night before I came over to the residential unit was a completely sleepless night because of the nervousness caused by the newness of the residential program. The other seventeen nights were spent in some state of limbo, in which I did not sleep enough to go into REM sleep. I never really "fell" asleep. Some of my addict friends said that my brain was going through some sort of synaptic wash and that was why I wasn't sleeping.

On day three in Residential, I saw the psychiatrist and told her about my sleep problems. She ordered a Seroquel for me, and we spent the next hour talking about my interest in Henry VIII. Seems she had an interest too. I saw her on day 11 and told her I still wasn't sleeping and hadn't slept for twelve nights—could she please help? She ordered me another Seroquel, and we spent the remaining hour talking about Anne Boleyn. Seroquel is given to people to induce sleep and thus eliminate psychotic breaks. This is important to know: mania can and will be brought on by lack of sleep. As a rule in manic depression, if the person denies himself or herself sleep, or is denied sleep by an external source, mania will be induced. This mania starts out harmless enough, but if sleep is withheld or impossible to reach, it turns into psychosis. Psychosis is a potentially deadly break with reality; the manic person, for example, starts believing that yes, as a matter of fact, they *can* fly—and then dies trying.

When I left the treatment center in December, I was in such a severe manic state that I scared my kids, my father, and my friends—but didn't scare myself. Before I left my brother's place in San Diego, I bought and gave every single staff member a lucky bamboo because it was called Lucky Bamboo and would definitely work magic for all. A week later I went to a restaurant with my son and two of his friends and insisted that after we eat we go to the nearest Volvo dealer and get each one of the boys a Volvo truck. Why? Because I had unlimited funds, and I was magic in my own mind. Why Volvo? They were supposed to be the safest-built vehicles. When the check came, my prepaid credit card had reached its limit, so my son's baseball coach, who happened to be dining there with his wife and kids, paid for our meal. That night began a three-year climb out of mania and into depression. The law applies: what goes up must come down. And all I did was come down. In the following pages I will attempt to explain this mental illness to you in a way that, hopefully, takes some of the meaninglessness out of the phrase "bipolar disorder," so that the layperson can understand just why I call myself manic depressive rather than bipolar, and can understand the illness a little better.

Hannah N. Walsh
January 2015

This is not another book about drug addiction, although it could be. This is not another book on child abuse—but it could be that too. This is definitely not one more book on bipolar disorder written by yet another psychiatrist, psychologist, neurologist, or drug counselor who has never experienced a manic episode or two. What this *is*, is a book about manic depression, more commonly referred to now in the *DSM V* as Bipolar 1 or Bipolar 2. *Bipolar* never meant a thing to me; the word refers to two poles, and both of them will kill you if you try surviving in below-zero weather; north or south doesn't matter. But referring to manic depression as Bipolar 1 and Bipolar 2 somehow takes the sting out of it, and the two terms are so innocuous or meaningless that a person who has never experienced mania and acute depression has no clue as to the severity of the illness.

I believe that the usefulness of the terms *Bipolar 1* and *Bipolar 2* is the way they break down the symptoms: To be diagnosed with Bipolar 1 disorder, you must have had at least one break with reality. This break is referred to as a psychotic break, and the very mention of the word *psychotic* usually conjures an image of a person slicing and dicing people or running with scissors with reckless abandon. Bipolar 2 disorder is found in people who have never had a psychotic break or episode but have suffered profound depression and/or hypomania. Hypomania is a giant step toward a psychotic break. People with hypomania talk, think, and move faster; they can be charming, require less sleep, may have a heightened sexuality, and are able to function, for the most part, undetected as ill by the rest of society. People diagnosed with Bipolar 2 disorder are no less seriously ill than those diagnosed with Bipolar 1. Both are at high risk for experiencing severe depression and suicide.

A noted talk show host from the 1970s did people with manic depression such a wonderful service when he described his own experience of the illness. Loosely worded, this most gifted man said this: You are sitting or standing in a dark room. You do not know how many days have passed, nor do you much care about the passing of days. You know only that you have been in this depression all of your life and can see no light at the end of this tunnel. There is a gun just out of your reach, and you could end it all with one bullet, but it would just take too much of an effort. You just do not have the energy required to get yourself up to walk the few short steps to the gun.

When we with manic depression are in this dark place, we honestly cannot remember a day when we were not depressed. We lose all sight of reality, and the happiest times are forgotten because this big black depression has taken our entire person over and is running our show. It is a dangerous show too.

So, Bipolar 1 describes those of us who have had a psychotic break with reality, while Bipolar 2 describes people who do not have a break with reality but do exhibit manic-like traits that are called hypomanic states. Bipolar 1 and 2 have something in common: a depression so severe that it can take you out of this life for good if you are not on some kind of medication. I know people will stop at this and say, "No. I have manic depression, and I am not on any medication." All I can say to those people is, "You're a better man than I am, Gunga Din."

Those of us who have been diagnosed with manic depression (which is how I will hereafter refer to this illness) live in fear of letting people know we have this illness, so not much has changed in how the public views this particular mental illness. We are experts at living in isolation, which we all do at some time or another. Isolation is preferable to coming clean with this illness because what would we do if people around us knew the level of our depression? We are masters at hiding our depression and we would never let ourselves be "caught in the act" of hiding what was really going on in our heads. Too much is at stake; namely, the two perceptions people have of us when they *do* find out. We are seen either as so tragically mentally ill that there is no hope and we are a danger to be around or, at least, as a big drag to be around because we cannot see the light that so many others see with relative ease. What would we do if people around us knew the level of our depression? What would those we joke with and are pleasant with at work or school do if they knew that we are so depressed we are barely living? Who the hell wants to be seen as mentally ill in the first place? It's the worst "shingle" to hang on someone. Oh, I guess sociopathy and psychopathy take precedence over manic depression in the *DSM V,* but I don't believe that people with a diagnosis of psychopath or sociopath ever feel as black and depressed as manic depressive people do. So, while being a sociopath or psychopath is worse because sociopaths and psychopaths *do* hurt people, they are rarely a suicide risk.

To someone with manic depression, the very fact that we have lived to see another bout of depression is, in a very sick way, a sign of bravery or at least accomplishment. We might have enough energy to get out of bed for a minute or two, but we never make the bed because that is just a Herculean task, and besides, we are going to wind up there sooner or later. We don't bother with showers, either. It's not the shower we mind; in a serious state of depression, the towel we would have to use to dry ourselves is just too damn heavy to lift. The towel must weigh so much more than we are capable of handling that just the thought of it keeps us from something as routine and normal as taking a shower. We absolutely know that there is nothing good about us, and we guard this belief anxiously, lest someone else find out that there is nothing good about us. Then what would we say? If we tell the truth, we are labeled mentally ill. If we are working in the outside world with this illness, the last thing we ever want people to know is that we have manic depression, which is known as a severe mental illness.

It has since been reclassified as a biological illness, meaning that the brain of someone with manic depression is not like the brain of someone without it, nor is it like the brain of someone with autism. People with this illness lack the synapses that distribute serotonin to their brains: These synapses simply do not fire as they do in people without manic depression.

I want to make something very clear here: if you have manic depression—true manic depression—and you're working in public, as I do, you are scared to death that someone, somewhere down the line, will discover your awful secret. You never want this personal knowledge to wind up in the wrong hands. Why? Because of two simple reasons. One lies in frequently heard responses like this: "Oh! I have an aunt that knew a woman who had bipolar disorder, and she's just doing great"— or she's crazy as a loon, but I never hear anything like the truth about the poor aunt, because as much as I hate to admit this even to myself, there is no chance of getting over this illness, and it may just get worse as we age. Or I hear, "Oh, everybody has bipolar disorder, so what's the big deal?" It seems that everybody is an expert today on bipolar disorder or autism or schizophrenia, but no one really knows what even one of these mental illnesses is like. Yes. They all know *about* autism, bipolar disorder, and schizophrenia, and as a matter of fact, they can tell *you* a thing or two you may not already know. Or—and I find this to be the most common response—they don't give a shit. You're just a strange person that has learned to keep your distance. When they *do* give a shit, you wind up telling them your life story just to explain the illness because you have finally realized that you cannot explain this illness to anybody without starting with your own life story. The illness is larger than your life story. You have told your story so many times by now that you don't want to do it anymore. It's exhausting. It's heartbreaking. It's time consuming! For the public, it serves no purpose because people don't know what it is but have already made up their minds that it's just something that crazy people get.

So here you have it. This is my life story, because I could no more explain this illness without telling my life story than I could explain why the sky is blue. We have had a plague-like outbreak of bipolar-disorder diagnoses. As I have already said, this term is useless and does nothing to describe the illness that everybody seems to have. If people are not being diagnosed bipolar, then they are being diagnosed with autism or the "new" schizophrenia. *Autism* today covers a wide spectrum of people diagnosed with this illness. I will tell you what I came to understand as autism. I learned about it at an elementary school where I was working as a second-grade teacher. For some reason, our shabby, poor, run-down facilities (on my first day of teaching, my husband dropped me off at this school, looked quickly around, and said, "Welcome to the Peace Corps") also housed Los Angeles County's disabled and severely disabled population. Within a few months, our overworked special education teachers were given one more student with autism. This child, who was maybe eight or nine, would start screaming in the classroom and then be quickly led outside and left alone on the ramp to his classroom. His scream was like no other I had ever heard before. It was not annoying, although it was very loud. It was the saddest scream I had ever heard from anyone. I wanted to fix him, help him, comfort him, cry and scream with him, but none of these silly things that I had been willing to try would have made any difference to this child. He was completely alone and isolated within himself, and that very loneliness was chilling to me. I asked Kathleen, his teacher, one question, and she described it so sadly and so accurately. Kathleen said, "Hannah, we cannot get through to him. I do not even know if he is aware of anybody else's presence. He cannot get through to us either, so he screams."

This was my first real encounter with autism. For me, this was the definitive example of autism, and it was brutal; however, today there are some people that are called autistic but can work, carry on two-way conversations, and contribute to society, and you would never call them autistic. At a NAMI (National Association for the Mentally Ill) meeting, I met a brother and sister who were labeled autistic and had extremely high IQs. I spoke with the brother, and he said this: "To be very honest with you, our cognitive ability is so much faster than the average person's that we are usually perceived as snobby and rude because we cannot stand the time it takes for most people to understand what we have just said." This is a far cry from the little boy screaming on the landing. He continued by saying, "While they are figuring out what we have just said, we have already moved on to three other subjects." His sister was just as bright. They had one thing in common that I learned after the fact. No matter how hard I tried to make eye contact with either one of them, I never did. So, I learned that night that autism has changed in its diagnosis today.

People don't get manic depression via a bump on the head or a high fever; at least I've never met anyone who has. I was born with this illness. Some people are under the false impression that manic depression is contagious. I believe my mother was born with manic depression, as was her maternal grandmother, who committed suicide. And while I do not know if the argument for manic depression is nature or nurture, or a combination of the two, or if it's solely caused by misfiring synapses, I do know that my mother's father was a pedophile and had sexual relations with both of his daughters, and my mother would tell that to just about anybody who cared to listen.

He shut her up for a moment by shooting her in the leg with his shotgun, with this admonition: "If you tell *one more person*, I will find you and finish you off." Her father was thirty-three when he married her fourteen-year-old mother. I find it so interesting when people say, upon hearing the age difference between mother and father, "Well, that's just the way they did things back then." No! That was straight pedophilia to all concerned: her mother, my mother, and my aunt Shirley were all victims of the thirty-three-year-old "daddy" who was a predatory pedophile. When my mother was seventeen, her father and mother drove her to a long-term psychiatric hospital in California, where she stayed for a solid year. The irony was that the father who sexually violated his daughter, and the mother who looked the other way every single time, dropped my mother off at the state mental hospital so that the state of California could "fix" her. My mother had shock treatments on a weekly basis. Mom was born in 1929, so it was 1946 or so when she spent that year in a facility so frightening that the students who attend classes at this former state hospital swear that they hear people screaming, and I believe them.

My mom was just a fascinating person. I believe she was a sociopathic narcissist—what else could she have been with her parentage? She was always very interesting to me. Interesting and dangerous. She told my brother, Kevin, and me three stories about her stay at the state hospital. Only three, and here they are:

One of the woman patients was a professional classical pianist who killed a woman in a fit of insane rage. Her stay was permanent, but so was her temper. For safety reasons, my mother—and every other inmate—was warned about this woman. My mother commented on just how many extremely talented but mentally ill women found themselves at this hospital. According to my mother, most, if not all, of the mentally ill and rage-filled women were remarkably intelligent. My mother must have also been remarkably intelligent to figure this out at the age of seventeen. She too was known as violent and dangerous, so she might not have realized the peril she was putting herself in when listening to this woman play piano. She played every single day on an old upright piano. I guess my mother either was naive or just really loved classical piano, because each day for that entire year, my mother would sneak into the "piano room" and hide just to hear this woman play. My mother knew all about violence because she was born right into it, but she risked her own safety daily just to hear this woman play. She never once felt that she was endangering herself, and the woman who played so beautifully might have known all along that my mother was in the room hiding, or perhaps she just didn't know or care. Whatever the case, my mother found at least one bright moment each day of her long, long stay at this hospital. She told my brother and me that all inmates dressed alike: a drab mid-calf sackcloth dress and shoes that were half-boots and made to last a lifetime.

The second story involves these very shoes and another violent patient—my mother. As I said, she was born into a rageaholic home and acquired the fierce temperament she needed to survive her own environment. I need mention only two words to describe my mother at age seventeen: violent and relentless. I do not look back at her life without compassion, because her life was so much worse than my brother's and mine, but that cycle of abuse is hard to overcome. One day, my mother told us, when the inmates were outside getting some much-needed fresh air, some woman happened to say the wrong thing to my mother, and my mother had her down on the ground with her right foot poised above her head. Her intention was to smash her brains in, and she would have done this if she hadn't been tackled by the orderlies. My mother was 5'7" and weighed about as much as a ten-year-old, but she had so much rage within her that it gave her incredible strength. This rage—the kind that knows no limits—made it necessary for four strong, big men to tackle her and tie her down to her bed. She never lost this rage. Ever.

The third story was interesting to me because, as crazy as she was and coming from the home life she was born into, my mother had a brilliant mind, an acute intelligence. She told Kevin and me that the women patients who were mentally retarded had the skin of teenagers well into their fifties and sixties. I do not know why this would be so, but I believed her and found her stories and interests fascinating. Somewhere between surviving her father and mother and life in general with the condition of depression and whatever demons kept her going, she knew the names of most of the flowers and trees indigenous to California and was a classical music aficionado. She was just seventeen.

Back to the genealogy. My mother had one grandmother that she loved. She did not love her mother, and just as much as she hated her own mother, she loved this grandmother. Her grandmother gave birth to my mother's mother, Wilma Grace, and to her uncle William, who was deaf and mute. She adored her uncle William, too. My mother's grandmother taught herself sign language. I do not know if she learned American Sign Language, but I do know that she learned how to communicate with her deaf son and taught him how to communicate with anyone and everyone. My mother learned sign language very quickly because she needed that one uncle to understand everything she had to tell him. Her uncle William loved her too. Sadly, though, her much-beloved grandmother committed suicide one day after wringing one too many chickens' necks. My mother told me this story about her grandmother over and over again, but she never told the story with any emotion and always ended this story by saying that her grandmother had wrung one too many chicken necks.

Even as a seven-year-old, I knew that something was not quite right with a mother who told such sad stories without showing emotion. She never reacted to this or any other terrible thing that she went through. Looking back now, I think perhaps she just couldn't feel good or bad emotions in the proper way, and it may have been my mother's only way of coping with that awful childhood. All I know is that she loved her grandmother and her uncle, and she hated her mother and father. My brother and I were told that our mother's grandmother committed suicide because of her severe asthma. My mom told us that she just had had enough of not being able to breathe, so she shot herself. My brother Kevin and I accepted this explanation until we were well into our twenties. We had one crazy mother and two crazy lives of our own because of her, so we always just took her word as truth until we were safe enough to hash the truth out from the false as we matured. Her grandmother was either a manic depressive or prone to severe depression. Today, she would be labeled as unipolar, which means she experienced only depression and no high manic episodes.

Whatever she had, she hung in there long enough to marry her deaf son to a deaf woman named Dixie. My great-uncle William and Dixie visited us at our house in Encino many times. I was just a little girl, and I was scared to death of both of them because they spoke with their hands and made utterances that were ugly and not like the English language. They scared me so much that I hid from them, but my mom was always a happy camper when her uncle visited us.

So, my brother and I are fairly certain that our great-grandmother was either manic depressive or unipolar. I know that my mother's mother had manic traits, because my mom told me about how her mother would sleep for weeks and weeks and then out of the blue would get up and clean the house like a crazy woman. My mom said, "like a crazy woman," and she was 100 percent accurate. My grandmother would be asleep for weeks and then be up for days and days yelling at her two daughters and cleaning the house with a toothbrush—an accurate display of manic depression's severe highs and lows.

Now for the maternal inherited traits. My great-grandmother had severe depression and took her own life because of depression and not because of asthma. My grandmother was manic depressive, and my own mother was either a narcissistic sociopath or psychopath—but then that's just my personal diagnosis of my own mom. She did exhibit manic-depressive traits in her later years, and if she was a true manic depressive, then her manias lasted for years, while my own lasted for months. My brother, Kevin, has manic depression. I have manic depression, and my paternal uncle had manic depression. I wasn't diagnosed as having manic depression until my late twenties. Just as soon as I could put that label on myself, I went looking for every symptom in my own daughter and took her to a psychiatrist who specializes in children and psychiatric disorders so he could put the "real" label on Victoria. At thirteen years old, my daughter was falsely diagnosed with manic depression, and I wish I had never insisted that she be tested so young. Of course she had manic depression, according to this specialist, but mostly because of what I told the specialist about my own mother and myself. He simply made all of my imaginings "true" when they might not have been true about Victoria at all.

Ten years later, I gave birth to Liam. I had to have an amniocentesis because I was thirty-eight. My husband, Steven, was diagnosed with schizo-affective disorder right before Liam was born. I was asked if there was any mental illness in the family, and I told the truth, so a geneticist was called in for a patient–doctor conference during the amnio. This was almost as bad as my insisting on having my daughter labeled as manic depressive, because this doctor had statistics and facts, and more statistics and more facts, and the geneticist reminded me, twenty weeks pregnant and crazy with excitement and happiness, of just how bad this poor baby had it with Steven and me as his parents. The geneticist gave some ridiculously high probability of Liam having schizophrenia, manic depression, severe depression, or any and all psychiatric illnesses known in 1994. I could not accept this diagnosis, and I never did. I definitely went looking for manic depression in my daughter but refused to believe what some geneticist said regarding Liam. I never went looking for anything in Liam except that which was good and right. He is twenty now and, to my knowledge, does not exhibit any psychiatric abnormality. However, my own didn't show up until I was twenty-one, so I pray that Liam never has to deal with this illness. Too bad I went looking for it in my own daughter! I know that my brother has manic depression *now*, but neither of us knew what the heck was wrong with us. My brother left home at age fourteen, so I do not know when this illness showed up in his life, but show up it did, and my mother just thought my brother was a drug addict because—oh, we all are addicted to something in the pathetic attempt to somehow get out of being manic depressive.

As I said, my onset was at age twenty-one, and this is what "onset" means to me. I was born with inherited manic depression, and while I always showed signs of this illness, such as extreme sensitivity to light, noise, and smell, I was especially sensitive to noise. Any repetitive noise I heard in any one of the apartment buildings I lived in with my mother would keep me from sleeping or require me to shove endless wads of toilet paper or tissues into my ears to muffle the noise and allow me to sleep.

At that time, I was a student at California State University, carrying eighteen units, working a three-day, thirty-hour shift at a local restaurant in San Diego, and dating the love of my life, with whom I was having sex—much to my mother's disgust and revulsion. I was an honor student, and I was also in a play that rehearsed pretty much every day of the week for six weeks and then was performed for three nights. I was living on coffee, cigarettes, and Trident sugarless mints. I lost so much weight so rapidly that when my brother saw me, he cried. He pleaded with my mother to get me help, but I thought I looked just great, and my mom had to work, so I was free to have my first manic episode—also called a psychotic break. So, my "onset" was at age twenty-one, when I did indeed have a psychotic break, or what was commonly referred to back in 1978 as a "nervous breakdown." I wouldn't have another manic episode until I was fifty-four.

When I had my first manic episode, it was the first time in my entire life that I had the energy of normal people. I didn't know it at the time, but I had Hashimoto's disease—a disease that causes your body to attack and "kill" your own thyroid gland. I had no thyroid, or very little. I was an asthmatic and often sickly child, so when that manic episode hit me, I was in heaven! I was absolutely as thin as I thought I needed to be and for the first time in my entire life had friends, whom I made in the play. Before then I had moved so many times that I never settled any place long enough to get to know people and let people get to know me. I wasn't comfortable at all with anybody really knowing me, but the people in the play were the best and the most fun. We really felt like a family.

After living on less and less sleep and less and less food, I had a psychotic break while working at the restaurant one night. I was floating around the restaurant, talking to all my personal buddies, and I felt I was the most delightful person you could ever know. But I also thought that all the customers in the restaurant that night were also the most delightful people I could ever know. Some of these people were Gypsies originally from Hungary, and in truth, it was very lucky that they liked me in that ever-loving and embracing manic state, because they were hard to get to know, for the most part, and, some said, very dangerous. I had an order for a bowl of clam chowder, and I spilt some on my forearm. The soup was so hot that the skin on my arm started to bubble. I didn't feel a thing and continued working because it was so much fun. Very soon after my arm was cooking, I was sent home. I thought, "Great. I can go hang out with my fun friends from the play." It was close to three in the morning. I got into my car and made it to

Chandler Street. Luckily for me, there was a night crew of city workers making repairs to the street. They had great big lights that I was sure were studio lights—like the Klieg lights of the many plays I had been in. I was completely sure that they knew who I was because they were filming my incredibly fascinating and completely useful life story. Still wearing my waitress uniform—which was also a very lucky thing—I sat under a very bright light while the workmen "filmed" me. One came over and saw that I was in bad shape, and he called the police. This kind workman asked me where I lived, and I could not remember, so I could not tell him. I was so very lost in every respect. When the police arrived, one officer asked me if I could tell him my address, and I couldn't. He took my license and got the address. I couldn't tell him who I lived with, because in this heightened state of mania, I knew there was something not right, but it wasn't me that wasn't right. It was all the other "players" that were actors in my life story, and all the other "stuff" was just that: stuff that was boring and getting in the way of my incredible life story that was being filmed at all times. When we got to my apartment, my mother opened the door and said, "Yes, officers. I've been expecting this for a while now." I do not know what my mother was expecting, but the police officer declared her a fit parent to leave me with, and that he did.

I was an adult, but not to my mother. She had already convinced me that I could never make it on my own, so I lived with her and never thought about living on my own or having enough guts to leave. My mother was very angry with me, and none too thrilled with the condition I was in. She immediately pronounced me to be drunk, on drugs, or a dope fiend like my brother. Kevin and I were not drug fiends per se, but we did take every chance we could to mask the manic depression that rendered us lonely and isolated "miscreants." I wasn't an alcoholic, and I wasn't on drugs; I was on nicotine, Trident sugarless mints, and caffeine, and that was it. I didn't need to sleep or eat at this point. That night my mother came at me with her big red angry face, her blue eyes bulging, determined to fix me good. She pushed me into a chair and looked into my eyes and said, "You look just like Mary." I didn't look a thing like Mary, who had been my brother's girlfriend a few years back, but I took the compliment anyway, which just infuriated her. She was absolutely frightening when I realized that she was dead set on "treating" what ailed me. So, the woman with the frightening red angry face and the huge blue eyes set out to "cure" me of my sexual proclivities, which were vile and disgusting to her; she used one of her favorite phrases to describe me: dumb cunt. She had begun calling me dumb cunt, whore, bitch, slut, etc. when I was eleven. I knew only what a slut was; while I knew that the other words she called me were bad, I had no idea what the hell they meant. She stuck with the lot well into my forties and her sixties. She determined that the whole "breakdown" was caused by sex at too early an age. I was twenty-one years old, but she was so very sick about sex that she drove me the other way for the majority of my sexual life. But that's another story.

Now she could finally tell my father and my brother that I was definitely autistic, or just mentally retarded. She came so very near to ruining my life then, and whatever this woman proclaimed about who and what I was or would be was the opposite of what I became and am still becoming.

She was promiscuous. She would sleep with men for money, and once she told me that she had to prostitute herself in order for me to have a rhinoplasty done because she hated my nose. "Oh, God. You've got your grandfather's nose for sure," she said. My nose wasn't hooked until she broke it, but I never told anybody that she did it. I remember waking up during the surgery at UCLA. The surgeon was having a terrible time breaking the nose, and I opened my eyes and felt for my nose, and it was gone! What a feeling. He told me to close my eyes and stated right then that my nose had been broken at least twice, but I just let my family think I had inherited my grandfather's hooked nose. Before my mother passed away, she was saying so many nice things to me and about me, and she had done this all of my life. She would apologize. At this particular time she came out and said, "Your nose was never hooked."

Back to Mom's plan for my recovery. She was working downtown and had to go to sleep early so she could wake up early and take the commuter bus downtown. At night I had to sleep with her. She would hold me down with one of her legs and tell me that I was breathing too hard. Eventually, I became very practiced at syncing our breathing so that we were inhaling and exhaling together. She slept while I just kept on syncing our breathing. Now, I was a twenty-one-year-old woman. At no time did it ever occur to me that I could and should have stood up to her. Not once did I tell her to go to hell and then just go hang out with my brother, who at least would have protected me. I believed all she said about me—at age twenty-one, age thirty-two, and age thirty-nine. Night after night, I slept with her leg holding my body down as I synchronized our breathing. When she had to leave me to go to work, she would tell me that every single person who lived in every single apartment was watching me, and that if I tried to leave for even a pack of cigarettes (even though I had quit smoking during the breakdown), if I went AWOL, *all* the people living in all the apartments knew to call her at work and turn me in.

Yes. I did believe her, and I left only to go to the Vons grocery store up the street and buy tons of Hostess cinnamon crumb cakes. This was something that I would never have done without this disorder. I was doing things I would never do in my right mind and was not doing the right things that would be good for me. I sure did love those crumb cakes and went from 107 to almost 155 in no time at all. Of course my mother hated my weight gain, but I kept eating and was completely baffled by my weight going from 103 to 107 and then shooting up to 155. I was not in control of my body; my mother assumed that role for me. The days I wouldn't and couldn't go out, I would roam that small apartment like a homeless ghost looking for closure. Her method was never going to work. My brother, who was already a professional musician at age twenty-four, would stop by to check up on me—well, not on me but on my mother. He said he would call the police if she didn't get me to a hospital. She had been asking around—I guess at the water cooler at work—and maybe having conversations like this: "Hey, my dumb daughter, who is a Lolita, is absolutely off her tree. I think she might need psychiatric help for what ails her, but I can't be sure."

Someone mentioned the psychiatric facility at a prominent school. I do not know who told me this story—and it might be just that, a story—but in April of 1978, one of the most revered and respected experts on the illness … She earned all this reverence and respect the hard way: by actually having manic depression while earning her several degrees, on her way to becoming a psychiatrist specializing in manic depression. She completed her studies at the university all while having her own terrible breaks due to mania. I cannot stress this fact enough, because the lay population has no idea what it means to have manic depression and the resulting psychotic breaks. They are so bone-chillingly frightening. The hospitals people are sent to are full of more scary patients, and the staff is just as crazy as Nurse Ratched in *One Flew over the Cuckoo's Nest*. If you can cry your way out of this bad hospital, you are only getting ready for the next crazy hospital with more scary people and an even crazier staff. They are so very frightening that you are afraid to live and afraid to die. You are afraid to go outside but more afraid to stay inside, and the anxiety is so very complete that death seems like the only viable solution in the time of mania. This prominent doctor went on to write several seminal and completely necessary books on this mental illness we share. However, the story goes like this. In April of 1978 – when my mother called the university hospital, they told her that they had one more bed left. My mother did not respond quickly enough, so this doctor, who was in her own state of mania, got that bed, and I was sent to another hospital with a psychiatric facility for a truly memorable stay at my first psychiatric hospital. The terrible news was that the psychiatrists working at this hospital knew nearly nothing about much of anything, and I find it so very hard to believe. Had I been hospitalized at the university hospital, I would have been using the treatment solutions that this prominent doctor had researched and prescribed for the illness. I am at loss for a better description of just how important she was for people like me in 1978.

In my first hospitalization for manic depression, I was immediately given lots of Thorazine, Haldol, and Cogentin. If I didn't feel mentally ill going into that first hospital, I was definitely mentally ill coming out. The above-mentioned "meds" reduce a person to compulsive shuffling, pacing, drooling—in short, the meds make you look mentally ill. One thing all of my psych-ward buddies have in common is pacing without stop up and down the hospital's corridors.

I know that in 1978 they didn't know what the heck I had. One doctor told my parents I had "euphoric schizophrenia," which just sounds like manic depression to me. I was in one of the top floors and had a room all to myself. I had a large window overlooking the city, and I thought, "Damn. If I could just break out of here, I could probably fly home in an hour or two." That was my best thinking at the time. Even if I actually could have broken out and flown home, I still didn't know where home was. I had lost all worldly possessions. Almost. We usually had every item of worth locked up, but I had somehow been overlooked, so I still had my cool wrist watch with visible workings of the mechanism. Back in 1978 it was a beauty, and I lost it playing poker with the addicts. To be honest, when you are in a state of happy mania, you will give your last dime to a millionaire if he or she asks for it. That's how happy you are, or that's how happy and magnanimous I was in that state of mind.

The "inmates," or the people who were admitted to this psychiatric establishment, were not allowed to contact the outside world. I could not understand this philosophy, and somehow I managed to come up with a quarter to call home. I have no idea how I did this. I really needed to contact my father, once I found out that the psychiatrist handling my case load would be leaving for Hawaii shortly. He put the order in to pump me full of Thorazine, and I was scared for my life. Thorazine is such a powerful drug; on it a person is rendered absolutely helpless. No matter how hard a person tries to overcome this drug, it cannot be done. People begin to shuffle their feet and drool. The scariest part for me was when my pupils were so dilated that I could not read anything, no matter how hard I tried. I was very handicapped and scared, and I knew innately that this much Thorazine, Haldol, and Cogentin was so very wrong for what ailed me.

I believed my food was being poisoned, and I wasn't eating much. I did manage to contact my father, who came straight away. My psychiatrist, a Dr. Gold, explained how I was to be given Thorazine and Haldol and Cogentin until his return two weeks later. "When I get back, we can see how she is doing. How does this sound to you, Mr. Walsh?" Being an Irishman from the top of his head to the tip of his toes, he responded with: "Oh, hell no. I'm taking her with me now." The doctor responded with, "You know, Mr. Walsh, some children are just not cut out to be college graduates, and your daughter is one of them." Please remember that I was twenty-one years old and not considered a child at this age, but I was always treated like an idiot, so being referred to as a child was commonplace for me. Just that single mistake can mess up your self-esteem and your ability to self-regulate. I don't know of a better way of putting this inaccurate reference to my status as a human being, but that's all my father needed to hear from this man. I do not remember any other time in my life that my father got so very angry about what was happening to me. He always cared about me, but not the way he came so alive with anger at this doctor who had assessed me so harshly in the fifteen minutes he had spent with me during my almost seventy-two-hour stay. My father told him, "That might be well and good for you and your children, but not for mine. She is coming home now."

I was released with this admonition: give Hannah this medication twice a day in pill form. Dr. Gold gave my father the meds, and my father gave the meds to my mother, who threw them away because she didn't believe in drugs. Now, I do not like the drug Thorazine; however, if your mania has subsided somewhat due to Thorazine, the wisest thing to do if you want to stay out of hospitals is to take it, to keep you from getting too manic again. But the only acceptable drugs according to my mother were antibiotics, so she flushed my meds. Within five days I was "up" again and over at my brother's house. He was rehearsing with his band, and I started to dance and could not stop. He practiced for five hours straight, and I danced in another room for five hours straight. He told me later on that I didn't take a break to eat or to use the restroom or even to catch my breath. I just danced until he took me outside in his backyard and told me, in tears, that he couldn't fix me this time, that he didn't know what was wrong with me.

How Mania Feels and What It Looks Like

After I had the most recent "nervous breakdown," or psychotic break, at age fifty-four, I was hospitalized after getting out of the treatment center due to the fact that I hadn't slept for nineteen days. I put myself into that treatment center to get off amphetamines and Klonopin. This was so very unwise of me to do because drug rehabilitation treatment centers are facilities for addicts and not mentally ill people, per se. Of course, it can be argued that anybody with an addiction must have some form of mental illness, and I suppose that would be an accurate assumption. I spent three weeks at the treatment center and did not sleep for nineteen days. My first three days were spent in Detox completely off all drugs—including my psychiatric medications. At the time and in the treatment center climate, I felt rather good about going off of all medication. The whole deal at any detox and drug rehabilitation is to get people off drugs, so for me this included no amphetamines and no Klonopin and no Seroquel and no Zoloft. I do not know how many times I have gone off all meds on my own, just to prove that I might not need them. I mean, what if my diagnosis was wrong, and I really can function without any help from medication? This time, however, was brutal.

Not sleeping is a bad sign for people with this illness, and I knew I was in trouble after day six because I just could not turn my head off long enough to sleep. This treatment facility has great speaker meetings of Narcotics Anonymous and Cocaine Anonymous. In all, their 12-step programs run well and efficiently, and I have to say I have never heard worse stories of "what it was like and what happened," the speaker having been almost dead when he or she turned his or her life around. Every speaker was dynamic—so much so that I could not sleep from excitability. The "inmates" at the center attended one 12-step meeting every evening at either six or seven o' clock, and I would get so inspired that I could not stop thinking. After day six, I knew I had to sleep. I saw a psychiatrist three times and told her I could not sleep. She ordered my Seroquel, but by this time I just wasn't going to be able to sleep. Too many sleepless days and nights had gone by, so I told myself I couldn't sleep, and I didn't.

When I left the center, I was in full-blown mania. I was giddy and happy and ever so funny with my sister-in-law and brother. I had great ideas and, for some unknown reason, an unlimited supply of money. In reality I had as much money as an English teacher makes. This is a fascinating fact of people with this illness: we believe we are, for the most part, indestructible. Suddenly we have unlimited resources—mostly unlimited, and unreal, money. When the dust around my life started to settle, I asked my psychiatrist what people with this illness did before we had such a thing as money. Why did we feel we had an unlimited supply of money? I do not know the answer, but the psychotic break I had at fifty-four was financially devastating. The first psychotic break wasn't a financial wipeout, simply because I had no money outside of what I made at the restaurant. This time I had spent so much money and had written so many bad checks that when I "came to" I was in a terrible state—unpaid house payments, cell phones that had been turned off, and electricity that had also been turned off.

After I was released from the treatment facility, my two children watched me go through what was a very frightening time for them. They had never seen me like this before. Even my brother told my daughter that he didn't know if I was ever going to be okay again. Compared to the psychotic break I'd had at twenty-one, this psychotic break at fifty-four was so much worse! The mania went on and on and on, for months. So, what happened? I was sent to another facility to get "well."

The next hospital was awful. It was as bad as the hospital in *One Flew over the Cuckoo's Nest*. The patients were scary, the staff much scarier. I really do not know how psychiatric nurses do what they do for as long as they do, or why they are even allowed to do what they do. Some, if not most, need to get out of the field just to regroup. The night staff was great, and the day staff was frightening. Within a few days my daughter had to move home to take care of my father and her brother because I was hospitalized again. One of the other patients, who was my daughter's age, started to hang out with me. I could not shake him—especially when he found out I was the sister of his best and greatest and most wonderful—do you catch my meaning here?—guitar teacher ever. I am not my brother, and all this did was make me more paranoid. I asked myself, *What are the damn chances of me running into one of Kevin's students at this hospital almost ten years after the fact?* I guess the chances were good. He would walk when I walked and follow me around and try to talk to me. It was okay at first and then just annoying. I remember he asked me, with a gleam in his eye, "What is it like to be manic?" I still *was* manic, so I could be very honest with him. My answer was, "Hell. It is hell to be manic." This was not an explanation of what it *felt* like to be manic. I could not tell anyone back then what this mania actually feels like. But I can tell you now.

It brought on such extreme anxiety that once I was home for good, I sat in front of my computer daily, contemplating how I could end the extreme mania once and for all. I was no longer on anti-anxietals, and I could not see the end to the mania and extreme anxiety. This is not happy. It's not fun. It's frightening because you literally cannot stand being in your own skin. You can't sit still, and you can't walk around aimlessly, but I did plenty of that in that big house, which used to be full of people but now was just full of me.

Back to the hospital. I went to a class, and when I returned to the group, they said Duncan, my brother's former student, had left for good. I was so relieved, but he was back within an hour. He had been hit by a car and was in the hospital proper, getting a shot of morphine. Now, this happened to him twice while I was there. He would get out of the psych ward, get hit by a car, and then get a shot of morphine. The second time it happened, I said, "Hmm … what are the chances of getting hit by a car twice in one week?" One of the kids pulled me aside and said, "Hannah, he is a junkie. He throws himself in front of cars and lets himself get hit. Then he gets to come back here for his shot of morphine." I'd had no idea.

The woman with schizophrenia was not doing well, and neither were the other patients. If the meds we were waiting for were some anti-anxiety medication, the patients who needed them the most would start losing their cool. We would all line up for our meds and were most polite—until the meds didn't come at the right time. Some patients would get into a fight with the staff. Once I got into it with a staff member. I'd had whatever med withheld, but it wasn't that for me, because I was off anti-anxiety medication. What it *was*, was being aware of what the day staff would do to the patients. Why would they risk a patient's mental health by prolonging getting his or her medication?

On three separate occasions I was told by the psychiatrist that I could go home that very day. And three times that was taken away from me without my knowing why. I would place all my belongings in a paper sack, and the young staff member would take them out and have me put them away while she laughed at my disappointment and fear. I don't know why the psychiatrist would tell me I was going to be able to go home on three separate occasions and then have that taken away by some laughing staff member. I can't imagine what the other patients were going through on a daily basis. The security staff was corrupt and was fired. They restaffed on the day I did get out.

I had detoxed from Klonopin, a diazepam drug that is very bad for you, but at this hospital they ordered Ativan for me, another diazepam drug, and I told them "no" politely and then yelled at them to stop trying to give me Ativan. Their response was to get the orderlies to hold me down and give me a shot of Ativan. At twenty-one, when I was at the psychiatric facility in Van Nuys, I was tied down to a bed, and it was frightening. I kept saying to these orderlies, "Do not tie me down," and one of the orderlies laughed and said, "We'll tie you down if we want to." They gave me the shot of Ativan. I was fighting so hard against it because I had just spent three weeks detoxing from Klonopin, and I was clean. They took my clean time away from me just like that. Psychiatric facilities and rehabilitation facilities are not the same thing. Why did they need to give me a shot of Ativan in the first place? Because I complained about the meds being off schedule. I am not violent. I do not swear. I didn't shout. I simply complained about four times, and that's what happens to people who voice their opinions while mentally ill in psychiatric facilities. People who do not know this about psychiatric facilities should know this because it goes on every single day. We are controlled with medication or shut up with medication or dealt with through medication for the sake of the staff, very rarely for the sake of the patient, if ever.

When I was finally released from this hospital, I was still manic. I was at this hospital for about two weeks, and nothing really had changed. I was still not getting enough sleep. I had been hanging out with young people in their mid-twenties who were, for the most part, heroin addicts; or I hung out with the woman who conducted the art activities. The two weeks at this hospital felt like two years. On the day I left, I was so scared that I would *not* be leaving *one more time* that I stood with my paper bag full of my belongings at the front of the facility for an hour, waiting for my brother to get me. The kid who was his guitar student approached me and started yelling at me, "You're not going to go home! You'll be back with us for another week," which just increased my anxiety. I did get out and couldn't get away fast enough. When I was finally released from this hospital, I was still manic, and things did not get better yet. I was happy-manic at this point, on my way home to do marvelous things and to be greeted by my loving family. Those things didn't happen either.

At home I went online and hired architects to redesign my house. I got painters and plasterers and all sorts of people to design my dream home, which I had created out of magazine cutouts during art activities at the hospital. I had redesigned every room in my house with magazine cutouts and glue and paper and really saw this as a viable blueprint for the redesign. Between the treatment center and the psychiatric hospital, I had purchased round-trip airfare to Heathrow Airport to take my son, Liam, to Liverpool, so he could see where his favorite musicians grew up. I was out of my mind and spending money left and right. While at the hospital, the plane to England took off without us. I took my son and his two sixteen-year-old friends out to dinner with a credit card that had already been maxed out. My son's baseball coach was coincidentally at the restaurant that night, and he paid for our meal. After dinner we were going to drive to a Volvo dealership to buy the three young men Volvos. Why? Because I had heard long ago how safe Volvos were. They were simply safe, or perhaps they were the safest cars, and these boys should have one each.

My daughter, Victoria, had been at my house taking care of my father and son in my long absence. My daughter was alarmed at my mania, so she called my brother, who came out and told me I was too manic to be out of a hospital environment. I told him he was crazy and that I was doing just fine. The members of my Narcotics Anonymous meetings, especially my sponsor, agreed with him, and off I went to my second psychiatric hospital, for about a week. This hospital was the best by far, as far as psychiatric facilities go—I have been in only three in all these many years, but this particular facility had a definite program with different medications and meaningful activities.

I want to state here at this point that I had not had any trouble with mania or such severe depression since 1978. This doesn't mean I didn't have periods of depression and hypomanic states and that I wasn't put on and taken off many different medications to deal with my manic depression. I just never had a bad manic episode again until I was fifty-four. Prior to this manic episode, I had been a successful primary school teacher, and then a successful high school English teacher. I was the head of my household and raised my two children without a husband after eleven years of marriage, and without any monetary support from the ex-husband. I was strong and a dancer and played the oboe and had friends and other interests and was high functioning. That's what I learned they call people with manic depression or any other mental illness who can "make it" in the world. We are called "high functioning." I took care of two children and a nonambulatory father for years. I didn't date, because I was so very busy taking care of people and working. And for the most part, we thrived!

One Last Hospital

We were not treated as "mental" patients at this last hospital. There was just a better feeling there, and so much more healing there as well. The group I was with bonded very quickly. We spent Christmas and New Year's together, and all in all, the doctors were very good. My doctor was great. I came out of the mania, mostly, and finally went home. I was now off my anti-anxiety medication—Klonopin—and very anxious. My father had been moved to my daughter's apartment in Long Beach, due to the fact that I was not a fit caregiver. My son stayed because he wasn't at risk for being hurt, but my father had been completely reliant on me before the manic episode, and I just was not capable of taking care of him. His social worker and my daughter thought it would be best to move him in with her.

How sad! Today is August 11, 2014, and I just heard the news that one of the most fabulous of comedians and actors has died of asphyxiation—an apparent suicide. This star had manic depression. This is often a fatal illness, and yet so little is known about it. If I listed the "stars" who have died due to this mental illness, it would take pages. When celebrities do come out about their "bipolar" illnesses, I bless them for it because people take an interest in celebrities yet typically do *not* take an interest in the sixteen-year-old who is sitting in a high-school chemistry class contemplating suicide. Whatever light celebrity mental illness can throw on manic depression is a good thing. The bad thing is that celebrities and non-celebrities alike die at their own hands because of the depression.

The psychiatrist at the very last hospital put me on lithium on a temporary basis because over a long period of time my body rejects it. The lithium brought me out of the mania, but I was still very anxious, and now my household was very small. My father, who had been living with me since the birth of my son sixteen years earlier, was gone. My son, very active in sports and school, was mostly gone. I was on a long-term absence from my teaching job, so I was home alone day after day with high anxiety, but my psychiatrist felt that I didn't need any anti-anxiety medication. I suffered through life. As I stated, most days were spent sitting in front of my computer contemplating how to end my life without it looking like a suicide, so I decided to drive my car at a very high speed into a concrete embankment. Day after day, the play was looking better and better. I didn't really want to kill myself, because I have children; but I cannot describe the anxiety I had at that time. I was afraid of everything. I hated seeing anything that reminded me of the drug rehabilitation center. I hated seeing anything that reminded me of the *Cuckoo's Nest* hospital. My ex-husband was living with his mother in Oceanside, so he wasn't around for me anymore, and I was just so alone with this illness. I would drive Liam to school, and then if I wasn't sitting in front of my computer, I would sit on the couch in the living room and look out the window until it was time to pick him up from school. I spent hours in front of that window. I hated to be alone in that house, and I was afraid to go out of the house. I probably had some agoraphobia.

After a month of this, I made myself get out and walk every single day, and it was hard for me. I didn't want people to look at me or notice me, because then they might know or guess how sick I was. If I ran into a neighbor, I talked so much the neighbor didn't have a chance of asking me about myself, so I kept people away from me when what I needed was people to be with me. Steven, my ex-husband, said that I should go sit at Barnes & Noble just to be around people, and that thought just terrified me. I was so lonely and so sick. I might have been out of all hospitals, but the healing process hadn't kicked in yet. That was a long, long process; it continues today.

When I finally went back to teaching, I was off the amphetamines and the Klonopin, and I was having bad anxiety attacks. The students noticed. I had put on twenty pounds, and the students certainly noticed that too and made comments about it. I tried to focus in class, but I couldn't, so I went out on leave of absence again, to have my psychiatrist try another "brew" that would work. Nothing really did work. I was sent to another high school, and that didn't work either, so I went on permanent leave. Then I was retired from my teaching job because I never gained the momentum needed to teach and organize effectively. I just couldn't do the job anymore. The one challenge I could not overcome was the murder of one of my students. Another student died in a go-cart accident. I had recently lost one to cancer. But I lost Jesse to seven bullets, and my heart just broke. I went into shock and could not shake off the sadness. I was through with teaching, and I knew it. I loved the kids, but they needed a stronger teacher. I finally had to say I couldn't do the job anymore.

As a "retirement" gift, I took me and my daughter to Vienna and Budapest. I had all my medication in Vienna, so I was okay there; however, I ran out the day we left by train to Budapest. Within two or three days

I was paranoid, afraid of everything and everybody, and my body ached everywhere. Even my hair hurt. I felt I was moving like a woman of a hundred years. I was so very clumsy that as a joke, while in Budapest, my daughter gave me the name "Clunky Duck" to describe me. I was a nightmare walking around, but I did as I was told; so Victoria and I saw Budapest thoroughly, because to stand still or to sit was also excruciating for me. I cannot adequately describe the pain to you, but I know this much: when I do not sleep for days and days (and I hadn't slept for days even while in Vienna), the mania comes quickly, and the clumsiness and the stuttering to get the spoken word out clearly become major challenges. Even if I did muster up enough energy to *not* stutter, I had lost my short-term memory, making communication rather nonsensical.

This is a rather interesting "coincidence," but before I went into the facility, I bought a movie called *Conspiracy Theory*. If you watch this movie, you will see manic depression presented just like it happened to me; the actor playing the lead is a known manic depressive. I watched this movie with my two children after being released from my last psychiatric hospital. This actor displays mania in this movie so well that I am fairly certain he was manic while shooting the movie. When I walk while manic, my gait is forward, and I take short, choppy steps, because I am tripping over my own feet. I stutter so very badly that I panic because I have lost my ability to speak and thus to communicate, and it's a very scary feeling.

The body ache is the kind that comes after you have denied your body sleep and rest. It hurts and on top of all this, you are scared to death without any real reason. You drop things. You break things. If you swing your arms when you walk, you will swing them without control, causing your body to swing into hard surfaces. Your skins hurts. It feels as if it is stretched very tight, and it feels as if it is on fire. I don't how else to describe it. You break things without ever understanding just what the heck is going on.

This is the first time I knew I was manic. I had a phone session with my psychiatrist, who was trying to listen and help me. We both said, "I'm manic/You're manic" at the same time. This was the very first time I understood so very clearly that I was very manic. When someone has mania badly, the symptoms and repercussions are far more painful when that person is out of his or her "comfort zone." I do not suggest to anyone to run out of needed medications while traveling in a foreign country. I don't know why I do these things—and that should tell you something else about the disorder called mania.

Manic depression, or any other form of depression will probably never be cured, because pharmaceutical companies, along with psychiatrists, are making good money from all the antidepressants and antipsychotic medications. In my case, it has been *all* of the antidepressants, antipsychotics, and anti-seizure medications known to mankind it seems. I loved reading one actress's account of her manic depression, because it is honest, but while she takes one pink pill called Lithium that works for her, it has never worked for me. I also loved reading a famous talk show host's account of his manic depression, because it too is a real account of this illness; however, he now receives regular ECTs, or shock treatments, and that works for him. My mother got plenty of ECTs while an inmate of the state psychiatric hospital, and they sure didn't do a thing for her. I do not know how much real damage they caused her. This was back in 1946, so I'm pretty sure that ECTs have come a long way since then. What I have found to be true about the treatment of people with manic depression is this: not much has changed in the care and treatment of people hospitalized since my first "episode" at the age of twenty-one and, hopefully, my last episode at the age of fifty-four. I am confident that the treatment of the mentally ill has changed dramatically since my mother's stay at the state hospital, but I don't really know. I do know for a fact, however, that the staff of psychiatric facilities that I have "visited" still treat the patients of these facilities with nothing short of contempt. I do not remember the staff when I was hospitalized at my first psychiatric hospital. I definitely remember the staff of the psychiatric hospital in Van Nuys at age twenty-one. They did all but turn the high-pressure hoses on us.

England once had a house for crazy people called Bethlehem, or "Bedlam," if you did not happen to speak the Queen's English; we know, however, that *bedlam* means chaos and connotes despair, and still the treatment of the mentally ill has not changed very dramatically since the days of Bedlam. What I am trying to say is this: we are *slightly* better off with today's doctors, meds, and psychiatric facilities since the days of Bedlam, and since my first hospital stay more than three decades ago. I am hopeful that the treatment of the mentally ill will soon change dramatically, so that those of us with mental illnesses and need hospitalization won't simply be housed in a facility that dispenses drugs and not much else. That's all I can hope for.

People with manic depression don't ever want anybody without manic depression to find out, because we just are not fun-loving zany happy people *unless* we are manic, and then we are insanely fun-loving people that need to be locked up, because we just are not seeing the world as it is and our erratic behavior can be dangerous. (For example, once I was out of the last hospital, I was almost okay but still very manic and a danger while driving, so my car keys were taken from me lest I cause an accident or the death of someone else or myself while driving with one hand on the steering wheel while looking at everything I was passing in my car. I just wasn't a safe driver then.) This is the fear that drives manic depressives into drug addiction, sex addiction, love addiction, food addiction, religious addiction—oh, just *anything* to fill up that place in us that is empty and confused and alone and sad. If we are manic, we know the harm and damage we can cause ourselves and others due to a strong sex drive that will break every rule in the book to get that drive satisfied—for a moment or two. We spend money on everything for everybody—until we come down from the mania and face the truth that we are not rich as Rockefeller. Mania is not always absurdly happy. When it rears its ugly head, it can be vicious and dangerous. I have never hurt anybody physically because of this illness but have said things that were so cruel to my own son and daughter and father and brother that when they tell me exactly what I said to them, I cannot believe it. I spend so much energy apologizing for something I all too frequently do not remember. But I did say those awful things, and I can never take them back, so relationships can become very damaged.

I will be fifty-eight in December, and I am doing well. I am volunteering with at-risk high school students and taking flamenco dance classes and playing oboe in an orchestra and enjoying being a grandmother. I am on four different medications for my manic depression, and I am also back on the Klonopin and take it on an as-needed basis because I have an anxiety disorder. My hope lies in the future and the brain. Perhaps manic depression will one day be treated by tweaking that part of the brain that causes our synapses not to fire as they should—something as simple as that—instead of with all the experimental medications and the trials we have to continue with, not to mention the ECTs that are still available to us. This has been my experience and hope for those of us who suffer with manic depression. We have a long way to go in understanding and treating this mental illness. I hope that the future holds something good and tangible for those suffering with this illness. But I can only hope.